★ THE STORY OF ★
NAT LOVE

BY ROBERT MILLER ★ ILLUSTRATED BY MICHAEL BRYANT

Silver Press

*To my brother, John L. Miller, and the fond adventures
we shared growing up in Portland, Oregon*   RHN

For Immanuel, thanks for your help   MB

Text copyright © 1995 Robert H. Miller
Illustrations copyright © 1995 Michael Bryant
Map copyright © 1995 Claudia Carlson
All rights reserved, including the right of reproduction in whole or in part in
any form.
Published by Silver Press, Paramount Publishing, 250 James Street,
Morristown, New Jersey 07960.
Printed in the United States of America.
10 9 8 7 6 5 4 3 2 1

Library of Congress Cataloging-in-Publication Data
Miller, Robert H. (Robert Henry), 1944–
The story of Nat Love / by Robert H. Miller: illustrated by
Michael Bryant.
    p.   cm. — (Stories of the forgotten West)
ISBN 0-382-24389-7 (LSB)   ISBN 0-382-24393-5 (SC)
ISBN 0-382-24398-6 (JRT)
1. Love, Nat, 1854-1921 — Juvenile, literature.   2. Afro-American
cowboys — West (U.S.) — Biography — Juvenile, literature.   3. Cowboys —
West (U.S.) — Biography — Juvenile literature.   4. West (U.S.) — Biography —
Juvenile literature.   [1. Love, Nat, 1854-1921.   2. Cowboys. 3. West
(U.S.) — Biography.   4. Afro-Americans — Biography.]
I. Bryant, Michael, ill.   II. Title.   III. Series.   F594.L892M55   1995
978′.00496073′0092 — dc20   93-46287   CIP   AC

Author's Note

Nat Love was born into slavery on a plantation in Davidson County, Tennessee, in 1854. As a slave, Nat learned to herd, rope, and brand cows and horses—skills that came in handy as the West opened up for settlement and ranchers sought individuals to herd cattle from Kansas to Nebraska. After the Civil War, Nat and other African Americans were eager to take their place as American citizens. In 1869, when he was fifteen years old, Nat sought his future in the West and became, perhaps, the most famous of all the eight thousand African Americans who drove cattle up the Chisholm Trail. Nicknamed Deadwood Dick after he won a riding, roping, and shooting contest in Deadwood, South Dakota, Nat Love has become a part of American folklore and a legend of the Old West.

"I'll be the Yankee and you be the Rebel," said little Nat.

"No, you be the Rebel and I'll be the Yankee," his friend William said.

"It's my gun. I'll be the Yankee," Nat replied, as he took the stick away from William. "Bam, bam, I killed a Rebel," laughed Nat, pointing the stick at his friend.

Seven-year-old Nat Love was playing soldier. It was 1861, and the Civil War had just begun. Nat and his friends all wanted to be on the side of the Yankees, not the Rebels. The Yankees were fighting to end slavery. But the Rebels wanted to keep young Nat, his friends, and their families on the plantation as slaves.

Sometimes, little Nat and his friends would go out into the fields in search of the enemy. "Company, halt! Spread out men," Nat yelled. "When I give the order, charge. Charge!"

All of Nat's soldiers charged—right into a nest of bees! Those Rebel bees put up a good fight. They had Nat and his men on the run, all the way home.

Well, that was Nat Love! All his life, he ran straight into adventure.

When the Civil War ended, Nat and his family, along with the other slaves, were set free. Nat's father bought some land and tried tobacco farming for a while. But the farm didn't yield much tobacco.

The family needed money. Nat remembered that there was a horse ranch not far from where they lived. He went off to try his luck there.

The owner had two sons about Nat's age. "Your pop around?" Nat asked the boys.

"No, he ain't here," answered the youngest. "Who wants to know?"

"The name is Nat Love. I live down the road a piece. I thought your daddy might need an extra hand around here."

"We got some colts. If you can break 'em, we'll give you ten cents," said the older brother. He knew the young colts had the devil in them.

Nat looked at the colts and thought about how much he needed the money. "I'll do it," he said.

He climbed up the fence, jumped on the back of a wild colt, and took off. That colt jumped and bucked all over the barnyard. But Nat stayed on. Finally, the colt started trotting around like he was used to carrying somebody. The boys paid Nat ten cents!

Every Sunday after that, Nat went back to the ranch until he had enough money to buy his mother a sunbonnet and a pretty new dress.

With the money Nat made breaking horses, things began to turn around. Tobacco was making a profit at the market, and there was enough money to stock up on food for the winter.

"Mama," said Nat, "things look like they're improving mighty fine, now. What do you think?"

"Don't play the fox with me, Nat Love," his mother replied. "I see that wandering look on your face. I ain't never seen much of the world. Maybe one day you'll come back and tell me what's on the other side of the mountain."

Nat hugged his mother. Then he saddled his horse and headed west. The year was 1869, and Nat Love was fifteen years old.

All the years of hard work on the farm had made Nat's young body strong. It had given him a spirit that even a wild mustang stallion couldn't match. Loaded down with confidence, Nat rode into Dodge City, Kansas, like he owned it.

Everywhere he looked there were cowboys sitting in silver saddles on big prancing horses. They were decked out in their best clothes and showing off to beat the band. Nat wanted to be a cowboy, too.

He started asking people where to find work. "If you're looking for ranch work, sonny, there's a Texas outfit camped outside of town," someone told him. "Be there at 6 A.M. I hear they're hiring."

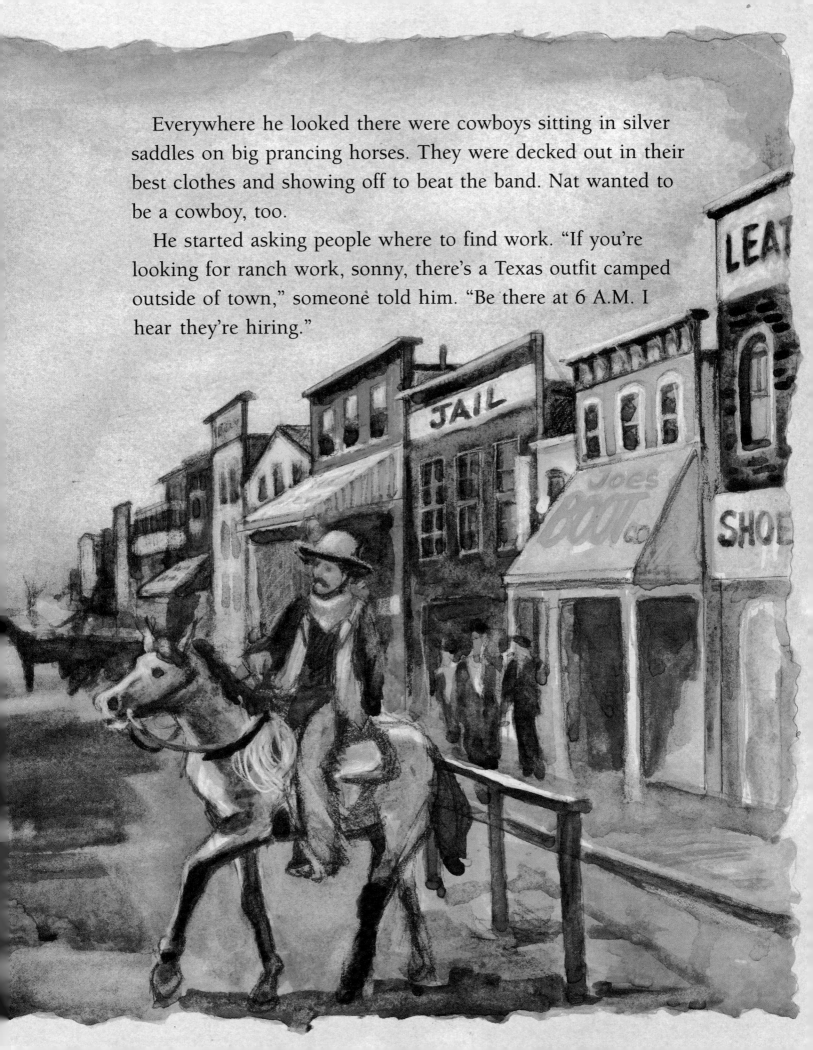

When Nat reached the campsite, he and the other hopefuls followed the trail boss to where they kept the wild horses. Turning to Nat, the trail boss asked, "So you want to be a cowboy. Can you ride a wild horse?"

Nat looked him straight in the eye. "Yes, sir!" he said.

The boss gave Nat one last look. "Bring out Good Eye," he said.

Good Eye was bigger than all those other colts put together. He was one of the wildest horses at the campsite.

"If you can ride him, young man," the trail boss told Nat, "you've got the job."

It took two men to keep Good Eye still while another man saddled him up. Nat's moment had arrived.

With all the courage he owned, Nat climbed up on Good Eye. When Nat was ready, the two cowboys let go. Good Eye shot out into the sage like lightning let out of a bottle.

He bucked and jumped. He threw up his head and pitched left. "Ride him, young fella, ride him," the cowboys shouted. Then they all watched Nat do something none of them had been able to do—stay on Good Eye. Finally, Nat rode him over to the trail boss and dismounted.

"You're good, son, doggone good," the boss told him. "I haven't seen riding like that in a long time. What's your name, again?"

"Nat Love, sir," Nat answered.

"You got yourself a job, Nat Love. We move out tonight." That was the beginning for Nat.

Nat learned all he could about the cattle business with the Texas outfit. He showed a natural talent for roping, riding, and shooting. As Nat's reputation spread, other job offers came his way. By the time he reached Deadwood City, South Dakota, some folks said Nat was the best cowboy in the territory. Others argued that other cowboys, like Stormy Jim, Powder Horn Bill, and White Head, were sharper than Nat.

Finally, the trail bosses decided to hold a contest. The man who could rope, saddle, bridle, and mount a wild mustang in the shortest time would be the winner. Nat Love was set to ride Glass Eye, the wildest mustang for miles around.

Everybody thought Nat had met his match. But if he was worried, he never showed it. Once Glass Eye was in place, Nat waited for the signal. The Colt .45 fired. Nat shot after the mustang like a wolverine after a weasel. It was something to see. He roped, saddled, bridled, and mounted that wild horse in nine minutes flat—three minutes faster than the closest contestant.

Nat's next contest was the one that caused the most commotion. Who would be the best shot in Deadwood City? The trail bosses set up targets. They marked off 250 yards for rifles, and 150 yards for .45 pistols. When the shooting was over, only two men were left to settle who was the best shot in the West—Stormy Jim and Nat Love. With a flip of a coin, it was decided that Stormy Jim would go first. He stood at the line with his rifle. He fired ten shots. When he was finished, eight bullets were in the bullseye. Then, at the signal, he drew his pistols and fired. Five of the bullets landed in the bullseye. That wasn't bad. Nat knew he had some slick shooting to do if he wanted to win this contest.

It was Nat's turn. He stood at the line and looked hard at the target. Then he picked up the rifle and did something that took everyone by surprise. At the signal, Nat fired from the hip. He placed every bullet right in the bullseye.

Stormy Jim couldn't believe it. But after he checked the targets, he had to agree with all the judges. From that day on, Nat Love became known as Deadwood Dick, champion roper and best shot of the western cattle country!

Nat continued to work on cattle drives. One time, as he was crossing Yellow Horse Canyon in Arizona, Nat heard the echo of an Indian war whoop. Bullets whizzed by Nat's head like hornets caught in an Easter bonnet. Suddenly, something that felt like a hot branding iron tore through his leg and into his horse. Bleeding and in pain, Nat passed out.

When Nat came to his senses he was in the Indian camp of Yellow Dog. He looked at his leg and saw that it was almost healed. "Why didn't you kill me?" Nat asked an Indian brave.

"You are a mighty warrior," his Indian friend replied.

Nat's bravery earned him the respect of his Indian captors. They offered to adopt him into the clan. But Nat longed to return to his life in the western territory. He knew he had to plan his own escape.

Late one night, Nat crawled over 250 yards to the place where the chief kept his stallion. He slipped a thin strap of buffalo skin into the horse's mouth to use as a bridle. Leaping onto the horse's back, Nat headed for the open prairie. He turned toward Texas and never looked back.

A free spirit, Nat Love stayed with an outfit only long enough to learn what he could. Like tumbleweed, he'd roll on to the next adventure. Nat Love died in 1925.

When old cowboys sit around campfires and tell tales of cattle drives, chances are they'll mention Deadwood Dick. Of course, they'll be talking about Nat Love, the greatest cowboy in the American West.